MORE PRAISE FOR BABYMOUSE!

"A new hero emerges in . . . Babymouse."
—**The Bulletin**

"Young readers will happily fall in line."
—**Kirkus Reviews**

"The brother-sister creative team hits the mark with humor, sweetness, and characters so genuine they can pass for real kids." —**Booklist**

"Babymouse is spunky, ambitious, and, at times, a total dweeb."
—**School Library Journal**

Treat yourself to all the **BABYMOUSE** books:

THEY'RE FRIGHTENINGLY GOOD!

BABYMOUSE

MONSTER MASH

R.I.P.

BY JENNIFER L. HOLM & MATTHEW HOLM

RANDOM HOUSE 🏠 NEW YORK

JUL 29 2009

AAAGGHH!

Published in the United States by Random House Children's Books, a division of Random House, Inc., New York.

RANDOM HOUSE and colophon are registered trademarks of Random House, Inc.

Visit us on the Web! www.randomhouse.com/kids
www.babymouse.com

Educators and librarians, for a variety of teaching tools, visit us at
www.randomhouse.com/teachers

Library of Congress Cataloging-in-Publication Data
Holm, Jennifer L.
Babymouse : monster mash / by Jennifer L. Holm & Matthew Holm. — 1st ed.
   p. cm.
Summary: A graphic novel following the Halloween adventures of Babymouse, an imaginative young mouse.
ISBN 978-0-375-84387-7 (trade) — ISBN 978-0-375-93789-7 (lib. bdg.)
1. Graphic novels. [1. Graphic novels. 2. Halloween—Fiction. 3. Mice—Fiction.]
I. Holm, Matthew. II. Title.
PZ7.7.H65Bam 2008 [Fic] 2008008433

PRINTED IN MALAYSIA 10 9 8 7 6 5 4

First Edition

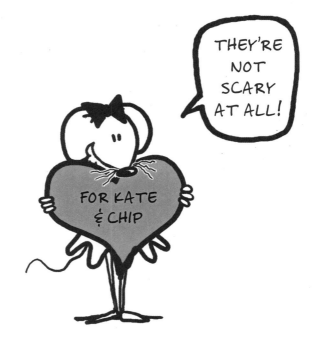

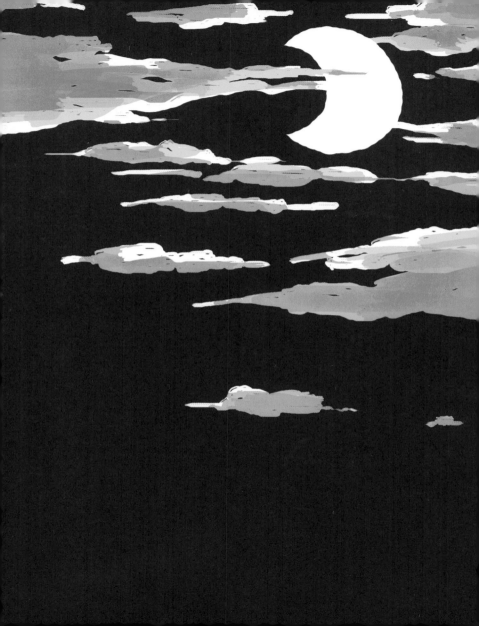

IT WAS SAID

THE MONSTER EMERGED

SPOOKY FOG

DURING A FULL MOON.

THE WISE

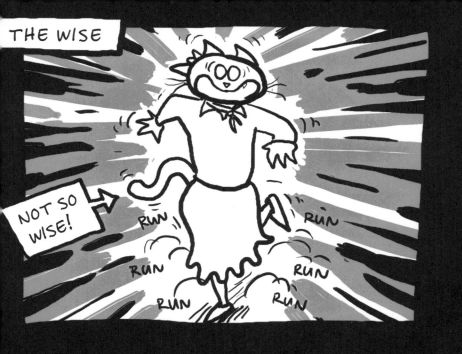

NOT SO WISE!

AVOIDED THE WOODS

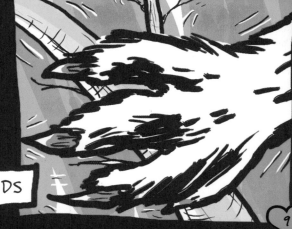

9

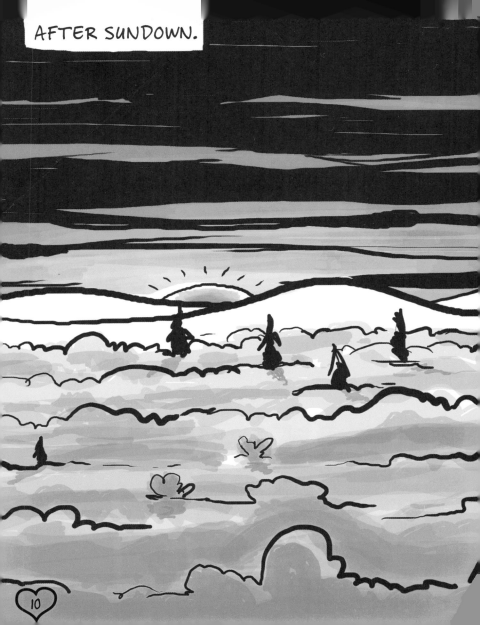

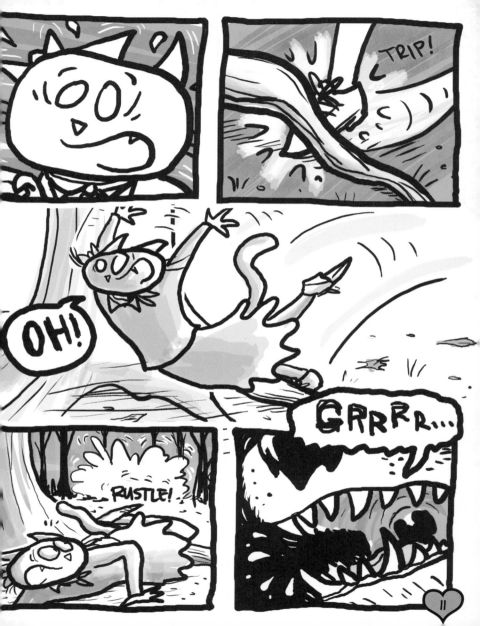

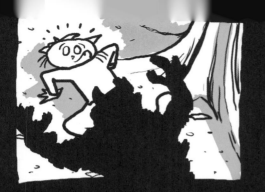

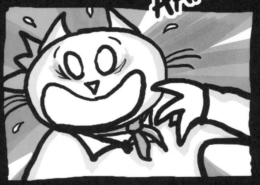

AAAAAGGGH!!!

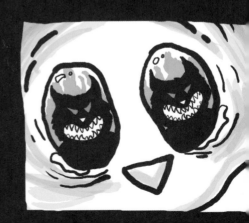

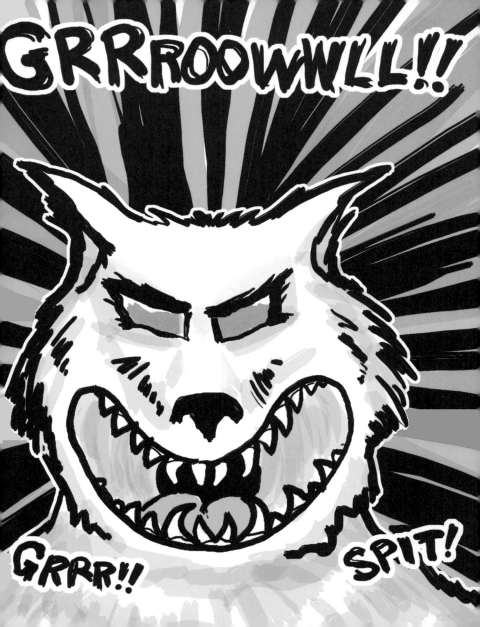

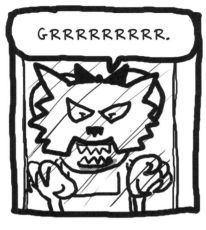

GRRRRRRRRR.

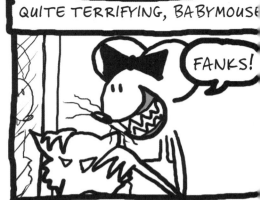

QUITE TERRIFYING, BABYMOUSE!

FANKS!

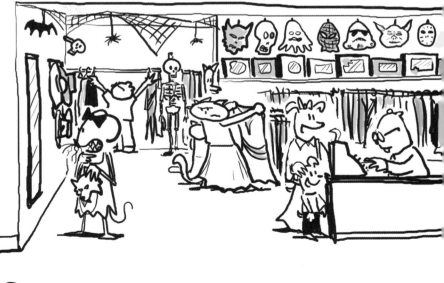

COSTUMES 'R' U

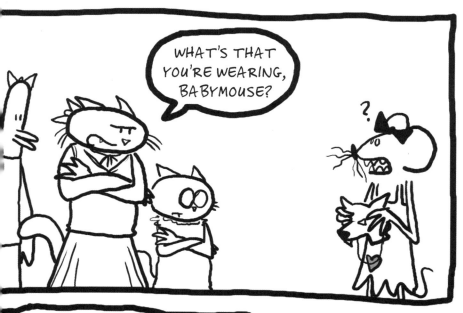

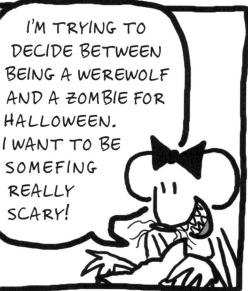

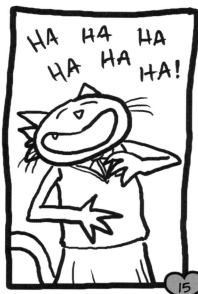

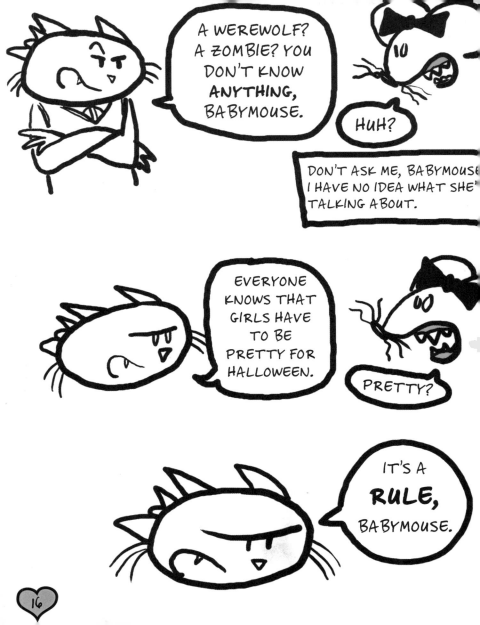

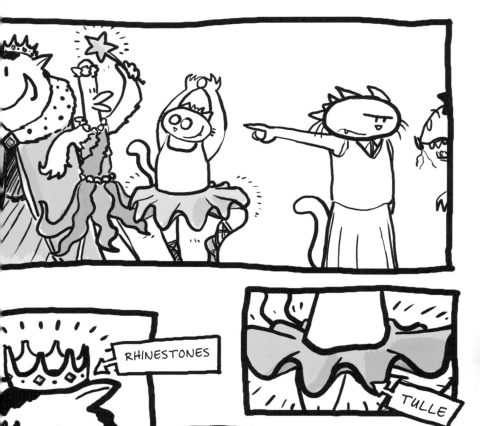

RHINESTONES

TULLE

GLITTER

17

ONLY BOYS CAN BE SCARY. DUH!

HA HA HA HA HA HA HA HA HA HA HA HA HA HA HA HA HA HA HA HA

MAYBE YOU CAN BE A "PRETTY" WEREWOLF, BABYMOUSE.

CAN I STILL WEAR THE FANGS

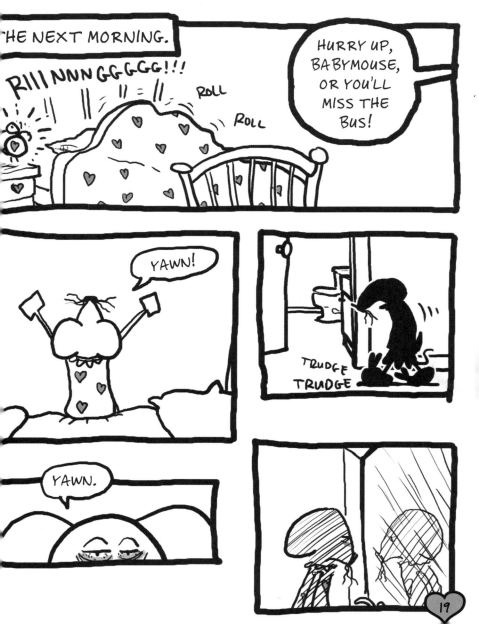

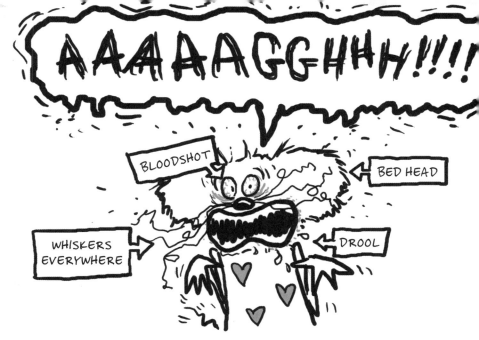

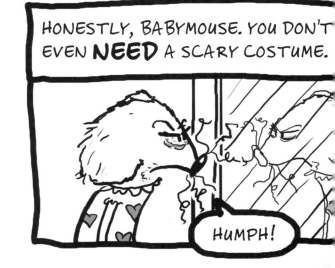

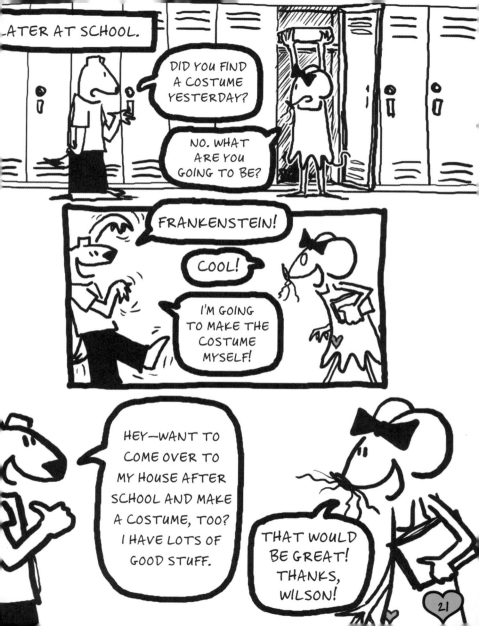

RINNNNGG!!!

SEE YOU IN CLASS, BABYMOUSE.

DON'T FORGET YOUR BOOK REPORT!

RIGHT!

BUT WHERE DID I PUT IT?

TOSS!

SPANISH MOSS

WHIZZ!

BLACK OOZE

UH, BABYMOUSE?

GULP!

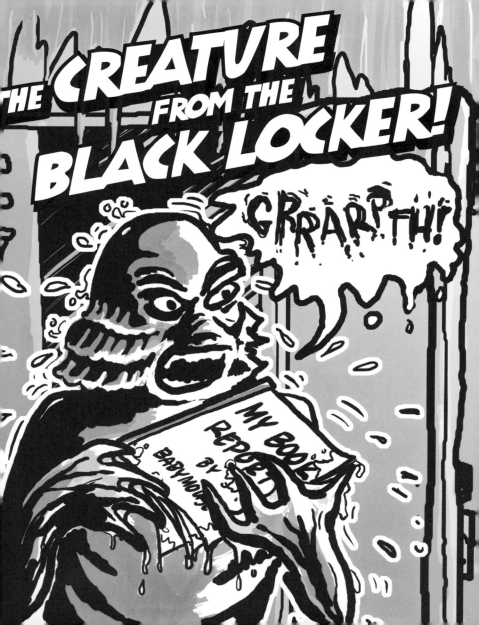

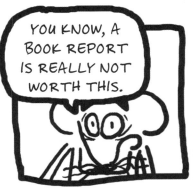

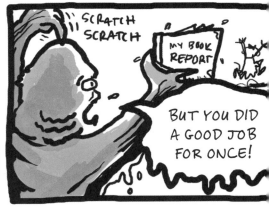

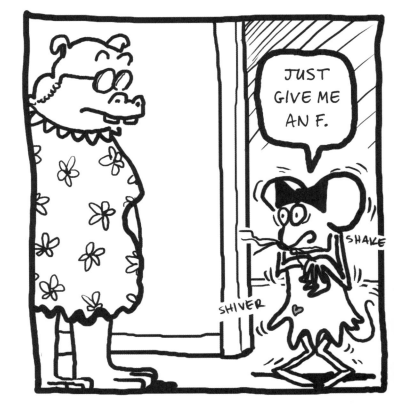

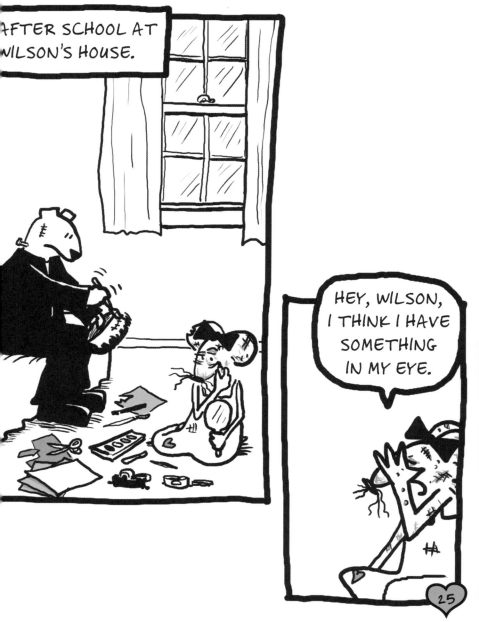

POP!

HA HA HA HA HA
HA
HA
HA HA!

LOVELY, BABYMOUSE. I BET THE BEAUTY-PAGEANT PEOPLE WILL BE CALLING ANY DAY NOW.

YOU HAVE NO SENSE OF HUMOR.

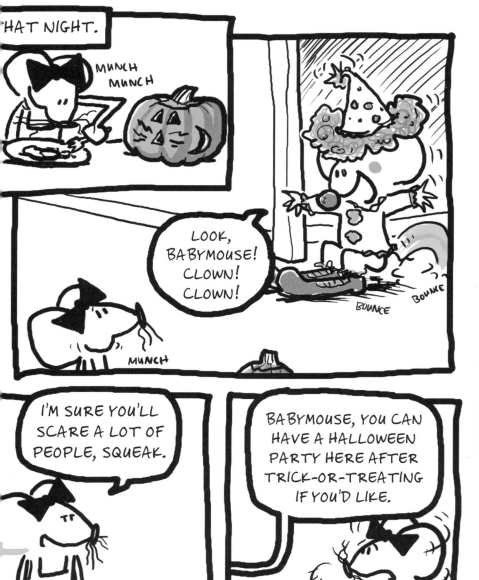

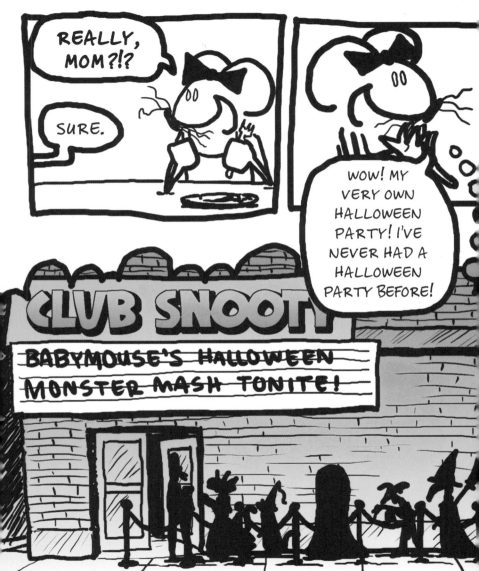

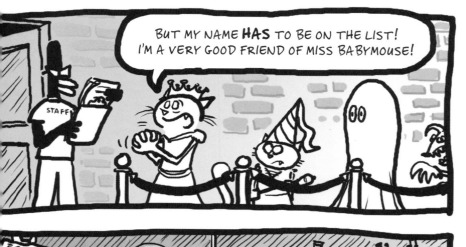

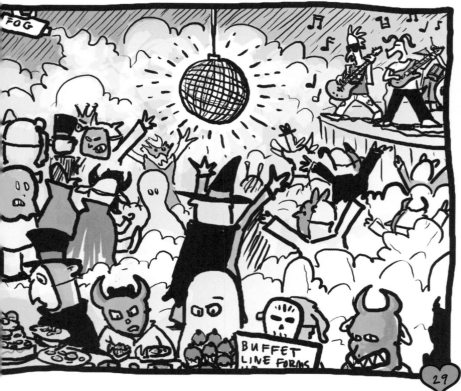

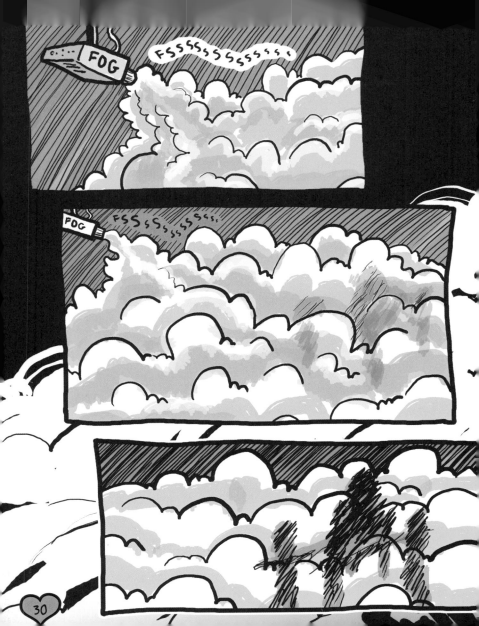

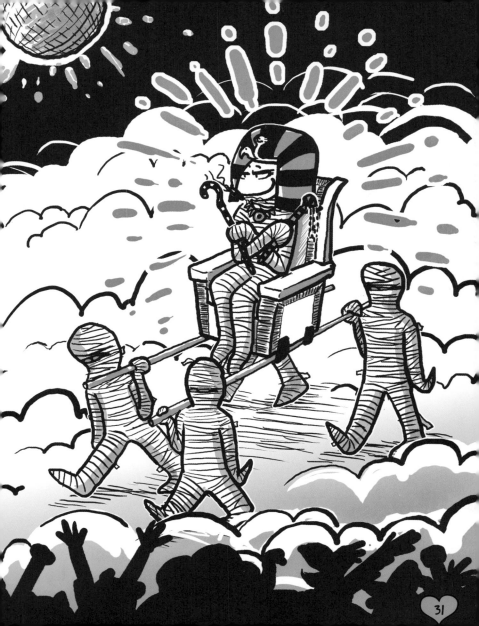

I WAS THINKING WE COULD HAVE APPLE CIDER AND CUPCAKES AND YOU AND YOUR FRIENDS COULD WATCH A MONSTER MOVIE.

GUESS YOU WON'T BE GETTING A FOG MACHINE, HUH, BABYMOUSE?

HUMPH! I REALLY THINK IT WOULD ADD A LOT TO THE PARTY!

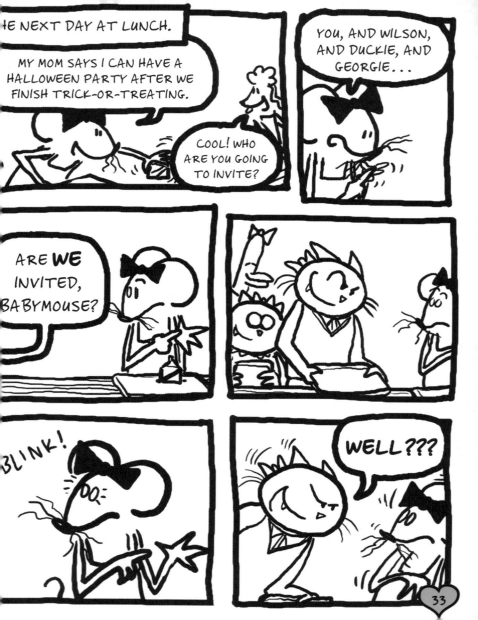

AH

UH

UM

UH

UH

UH

SURE!

IT WILL BE THE EVENT OF THE YEAR NOW!

YOU'RE **LUCKY,** BABYMOUSE.

BE CAREFUL, BABYMOUSE. REMEMBER WHAT HAPPENED IN BOOK ONE?

MAYBE SHE'S CHANGED? AND BESIDES— IT'S JUST A PARTY.

I DON'T KNOW, BABYMOUSE.

IT'LL BE GREAT JUST YO WATCH

34

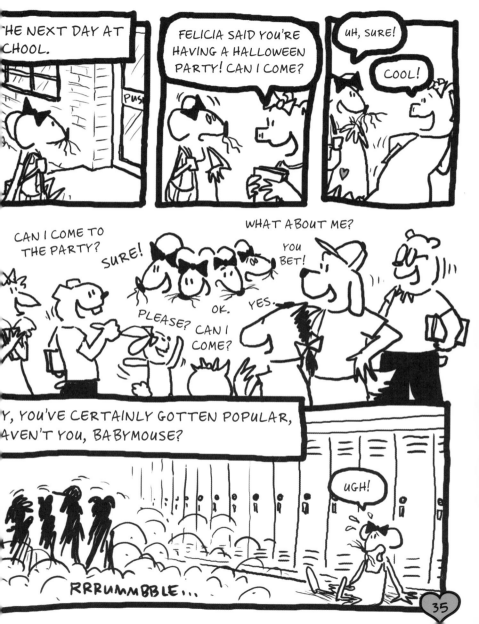

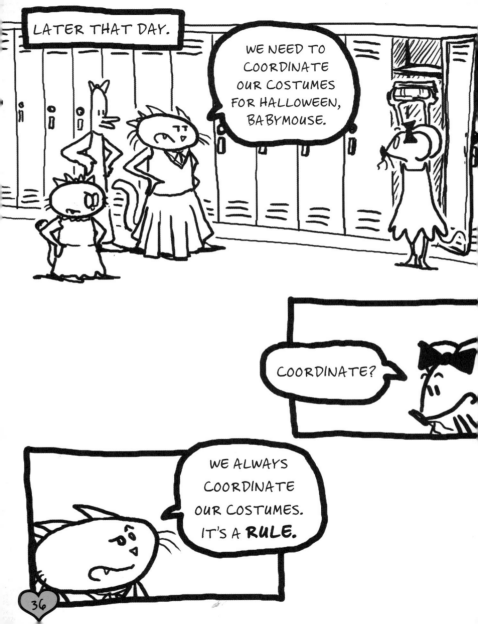

I'M GOING TO BE A BRIDE, AND WE ALREADY HAVE TWO PRINCESSES, SO YOU CAN...

MEOW MEOW MEOW...

DOUBLE, DOUBLE

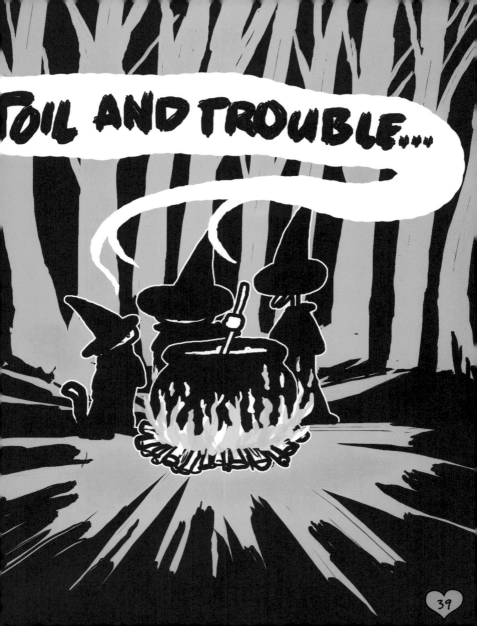

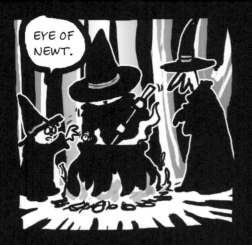

EYE OF NEWT.

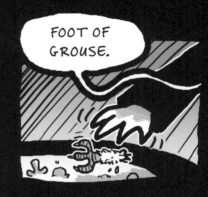

FOOT OF GROUSE.

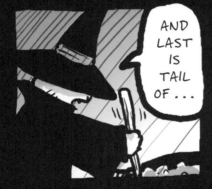

AND LAST IS TAIL OF . . .

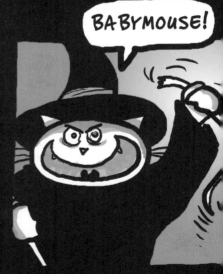

BABYMOUSE!

HA HA HA HA HA HA HA HA HA HA HA HA HA HA HA HA HA HA HA HA HA HA HA HA HA HA

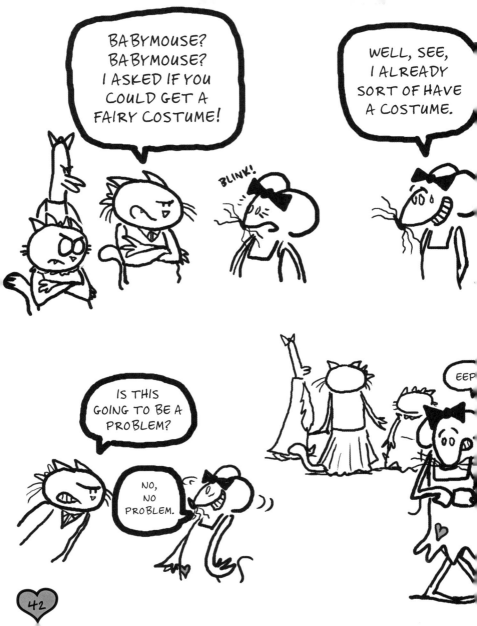

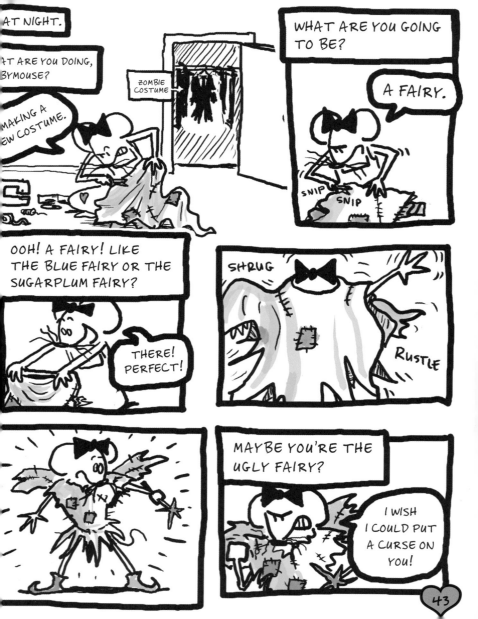

COSTUMES 'R' US

HOW'S IT GOING IN THERE, BABYMOUSE?

FITTING ROOM

ALMOST READY, MOM!

SLAM!

HOW LOVELY, BABYMOUSE.

YOU LOOK DELICIOUS, BABYMOUSE. LIKE A CUPCAKE.

THANK-

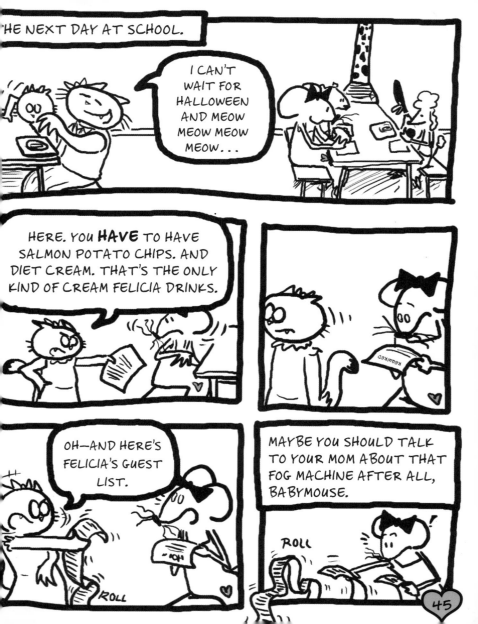

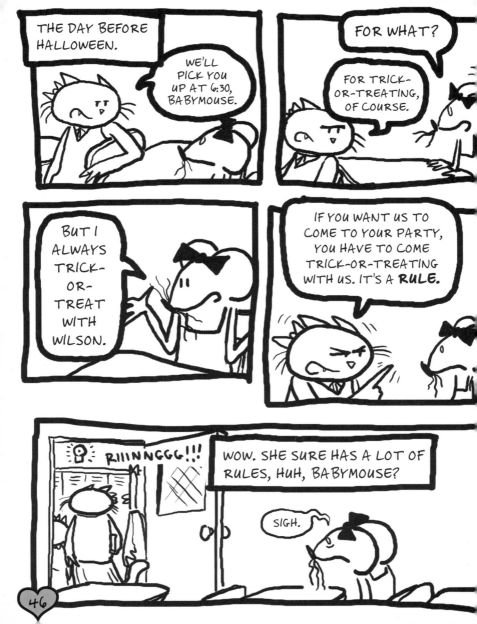

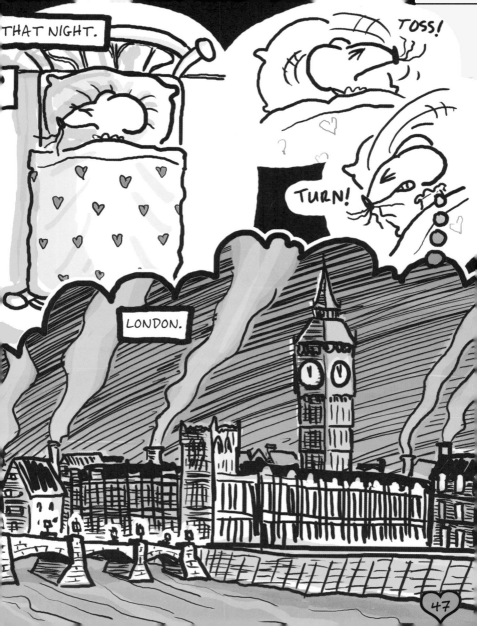

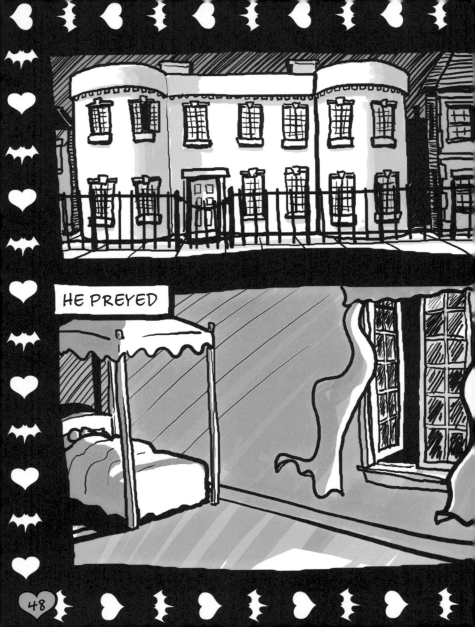

HE PREYED

48

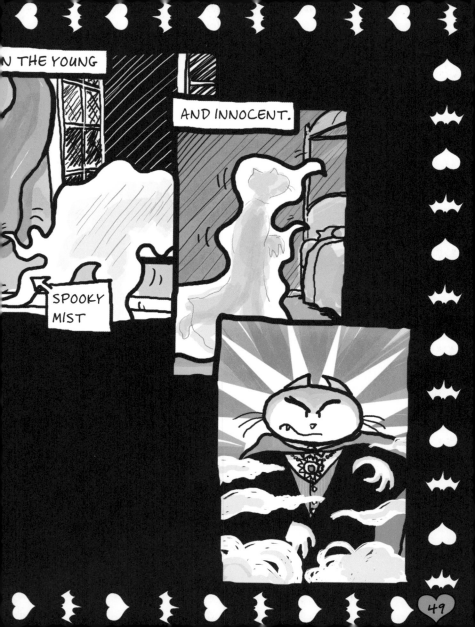

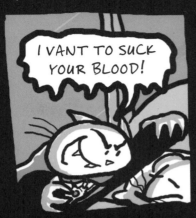
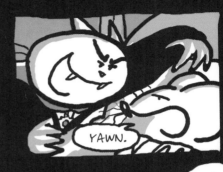
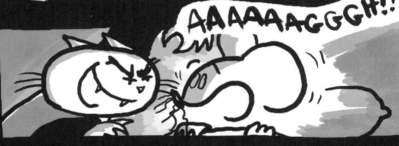
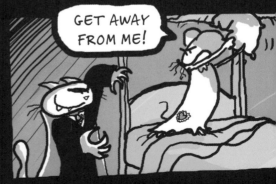

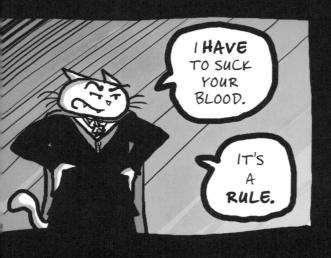

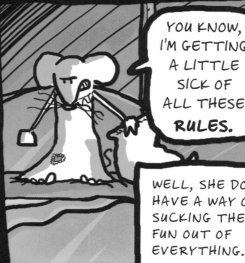

HALLOWEEN NIGHT.

RUSTLE

TUG

DING DONG!

THAT'S FOR ME, MOM.

SEE YOU BACK HERE AFTER TRICK OR-TREATING BABYMOUSE!

NOT BAD, BABYMOUSE.

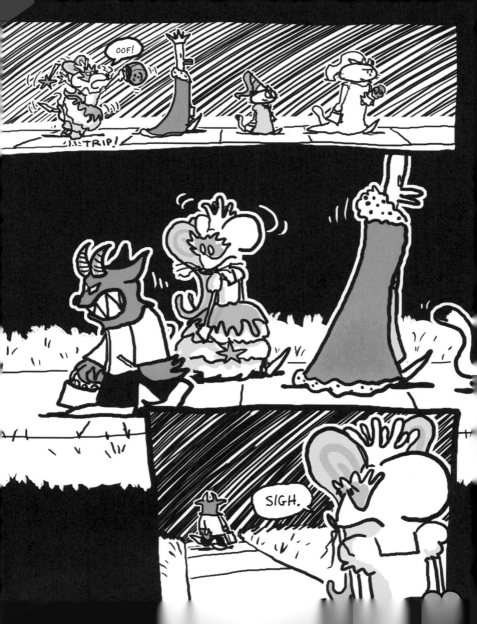

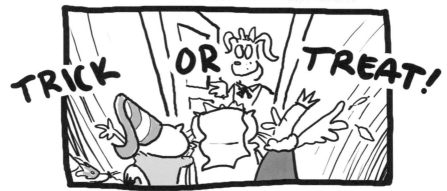

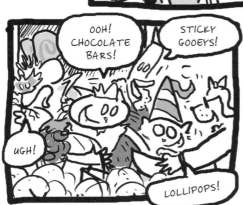

RRRUUMMMMBBBBLLE...

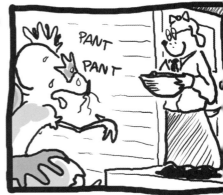

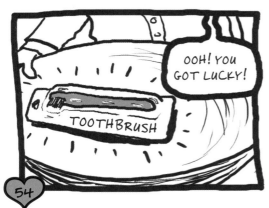

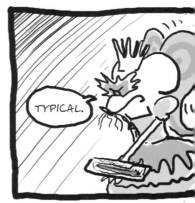

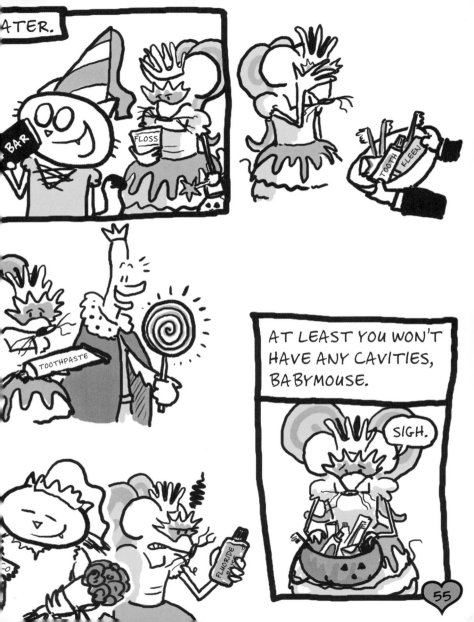

EVEN LATER.

WELL, OUR BAGS ARE FULL.

LET'S GO BACK TO MY HOUSE NOW.

NOT JUST YET, BABYMOUSE.

IT'S NOT CALLED **TRICK-** OR-TREATING FOR NOTHING!

TRICKS? YOU MEAN LIKE RINGING DOORBELLS AND RUNNING AWAY?

NOT QUITE, BABYMOUSE.

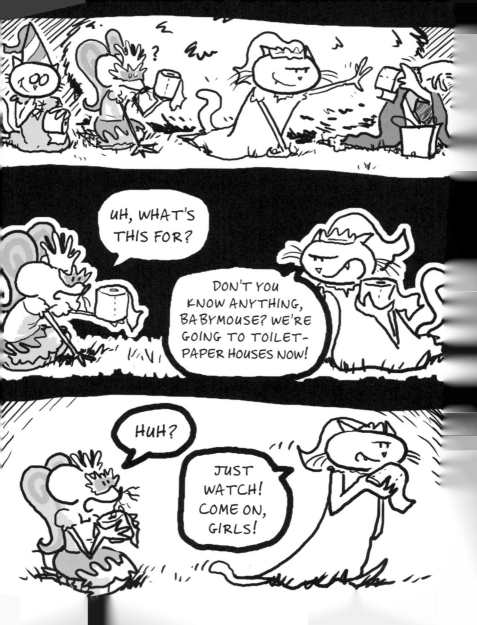

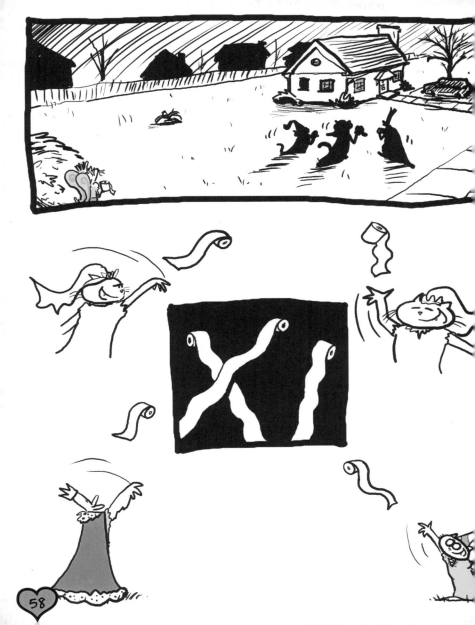

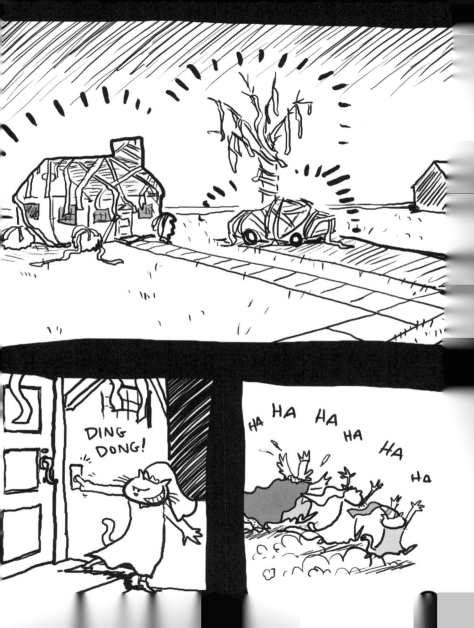

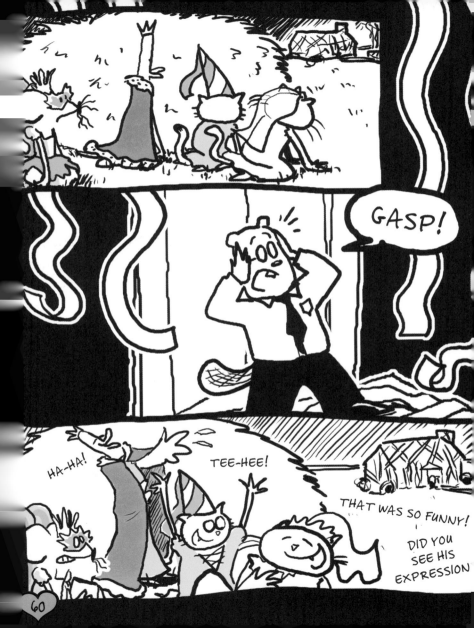

YOUR TURN, BABYMOUSE. DO THAT HOUSE OVER THERE.

GULP!

TIP TOE TIP TOE TIP TOE

BABYMOUSE— THINK OF THE TREES. BESIDES, WASTING TOILET PAPER LIKE THAT ISN'T VERY GOOD FOR THE ENVIRONMENT.

I KNOW.

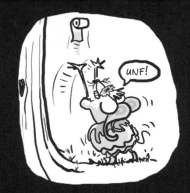

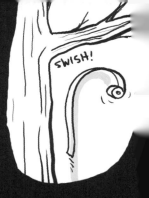

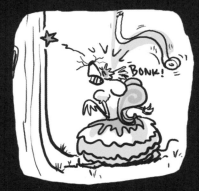

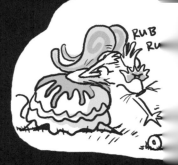

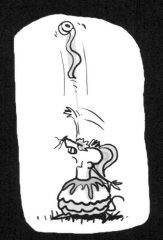

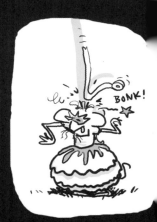

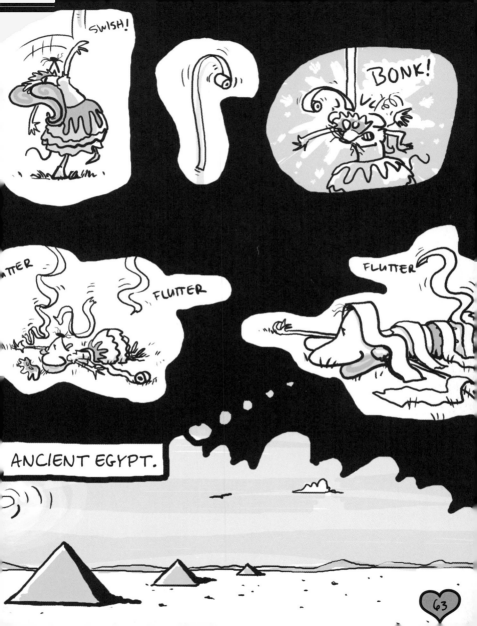

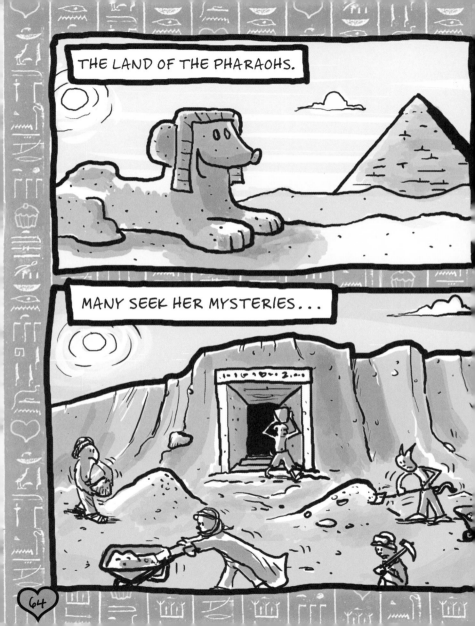

AT LAST!

AND HER TREASURES.

THE TREASURE OF BABYMOUSE-ANKH-AMUN!

I'LL BE RICH!

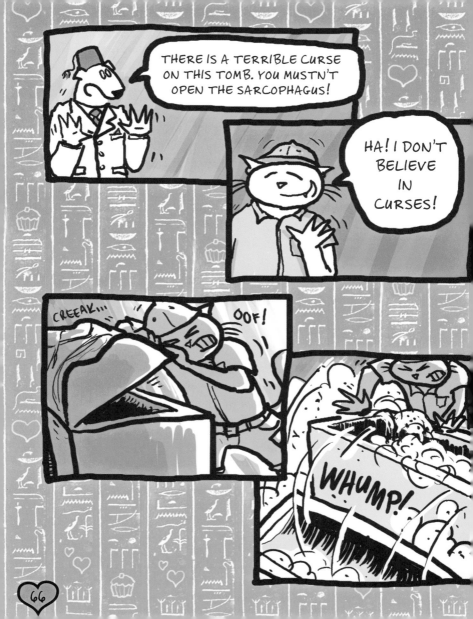

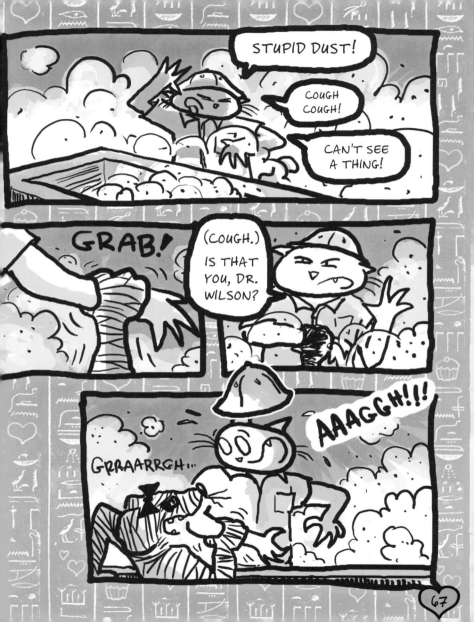

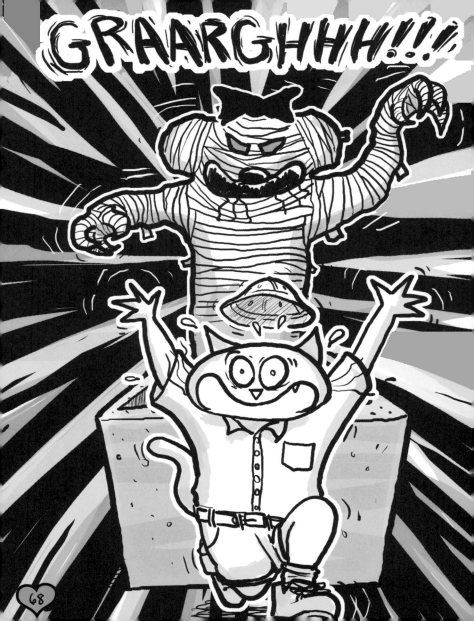

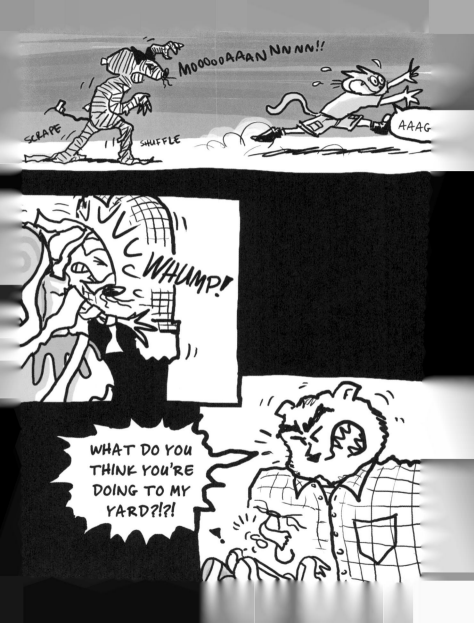

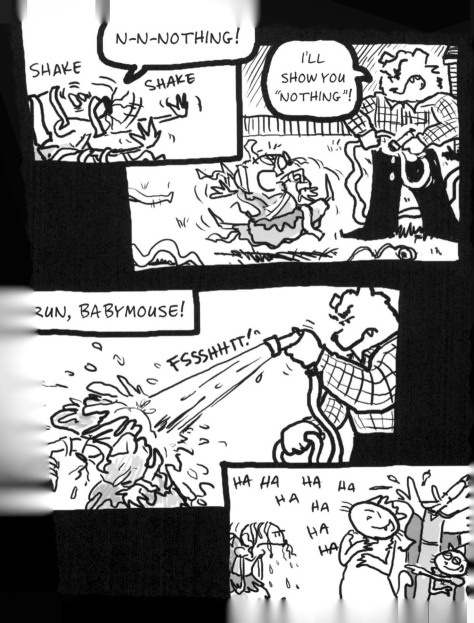

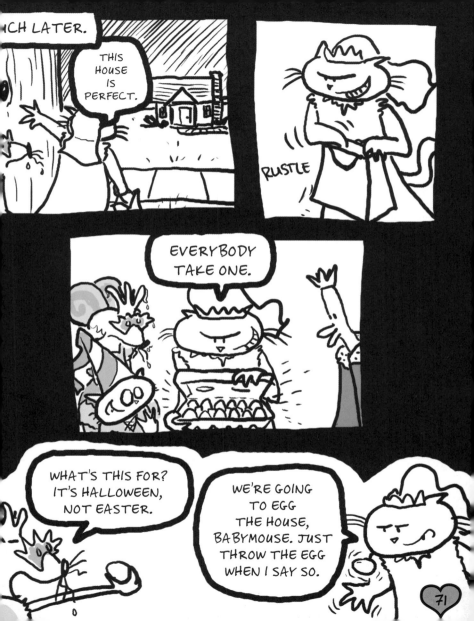

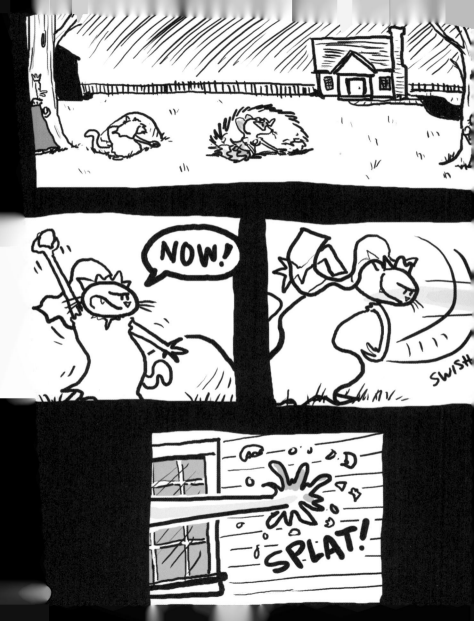

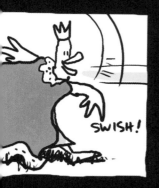
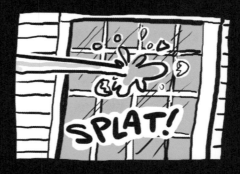
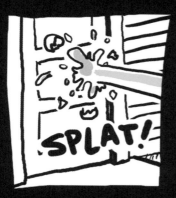
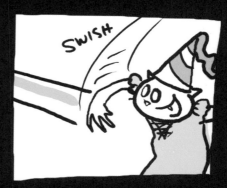
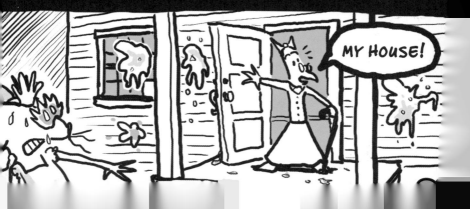

PSST! HURRY! THROW THE EGG, BABYMOUSE!

FLING!

SPLAT!

I USED TO REALLY LIKE HALLOWEEN BEFORE TONIGHT.

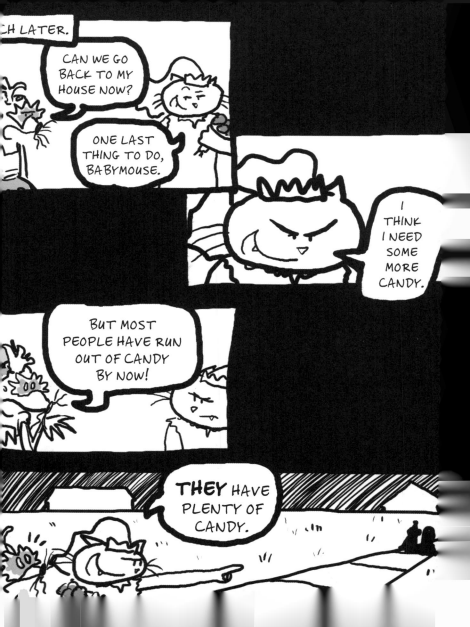

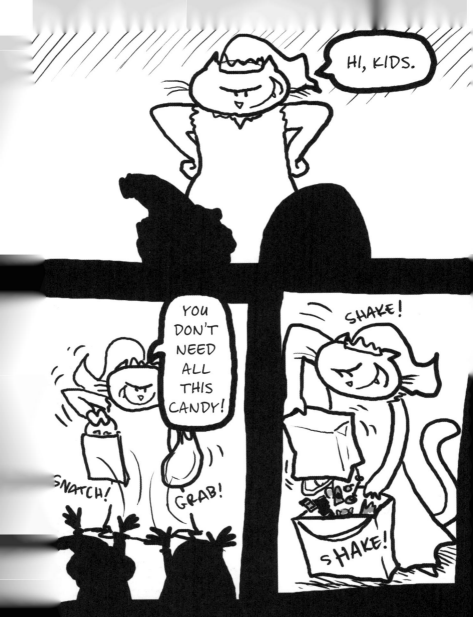

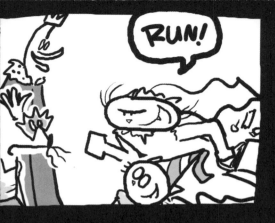

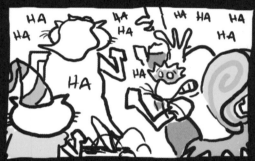

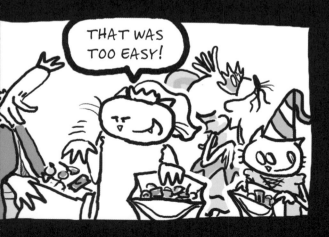

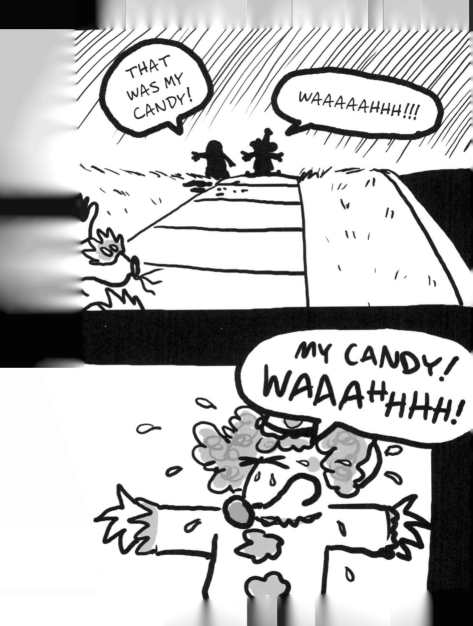

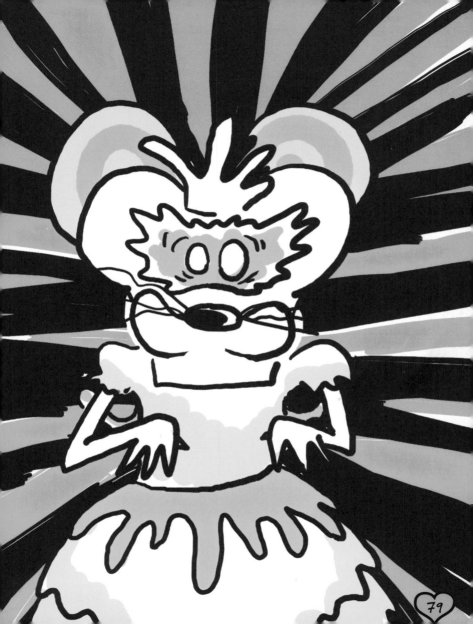

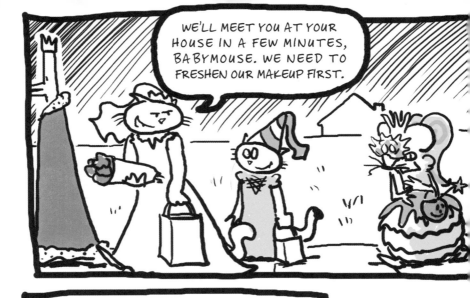

BABYMOUSE, I CAN'T BELIEVE—

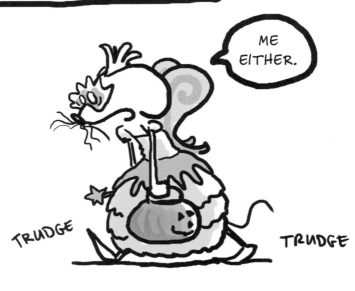

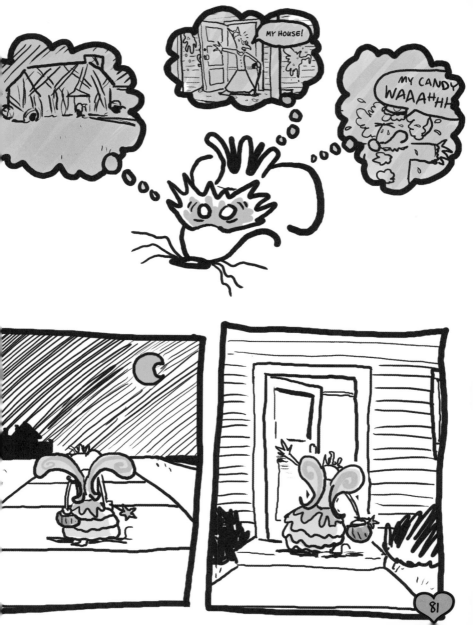

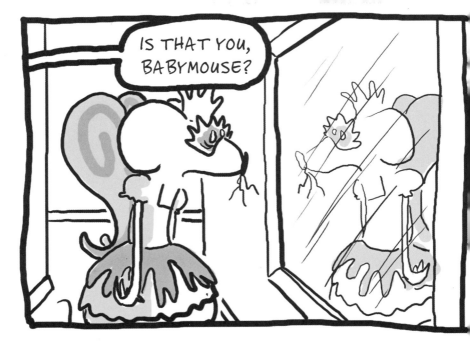

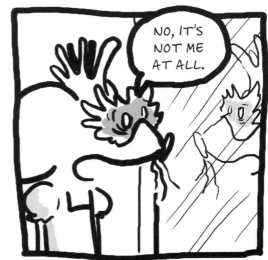

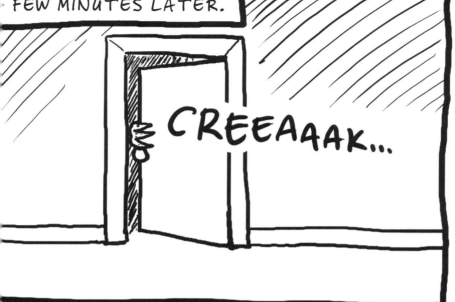

CREEAAAK...

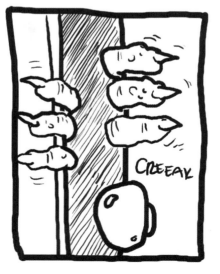

CREEAK

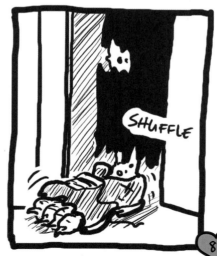

SHUFFLE

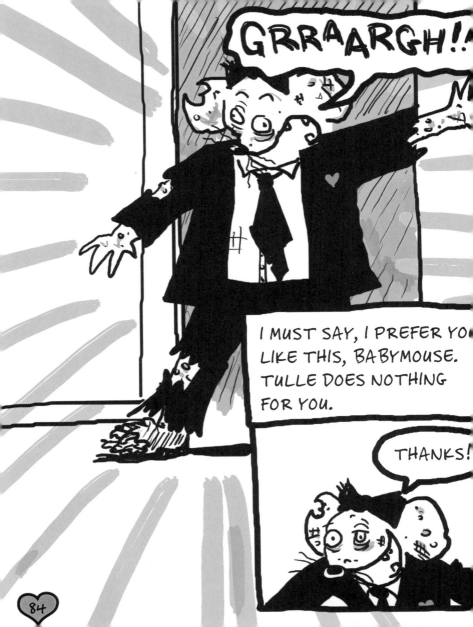

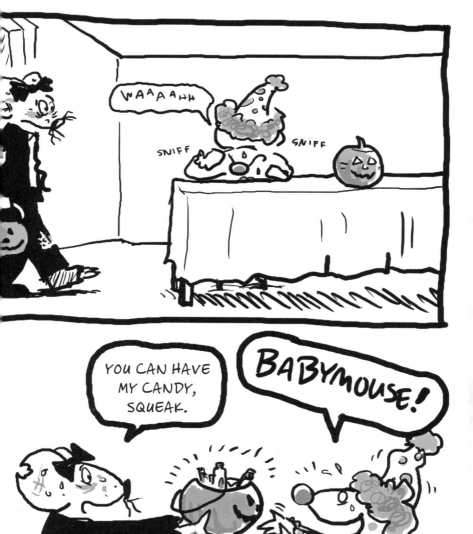

YOUR DENTIST WILL APPROVE, BABYMOUSE.

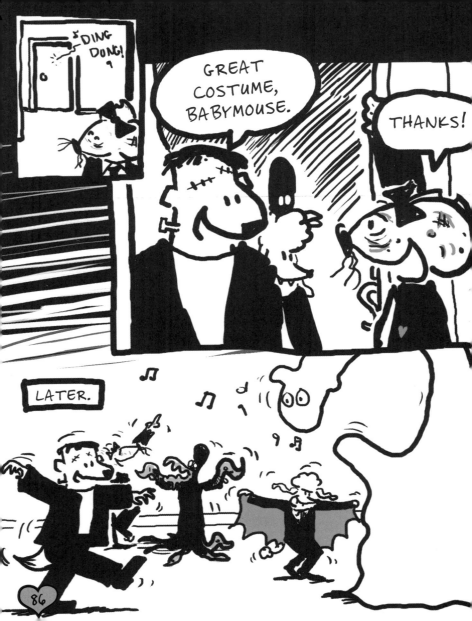

DING DONG!

I'LL GET IT, MOM!

WE'RE HERE!

YOU CAN'T COME IN WITHOUT A SCARY COSTUME.

SHAKE SHAKE

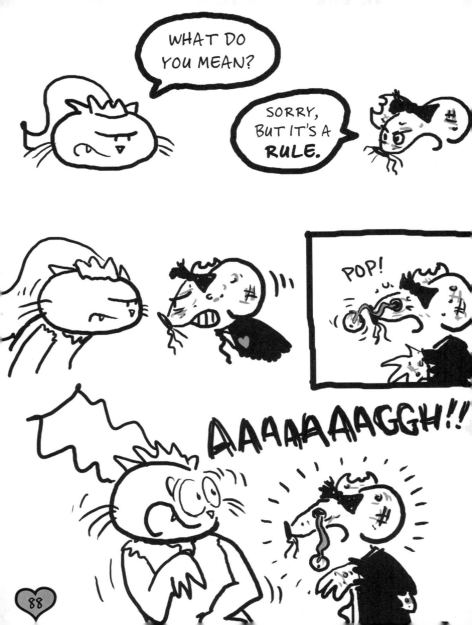

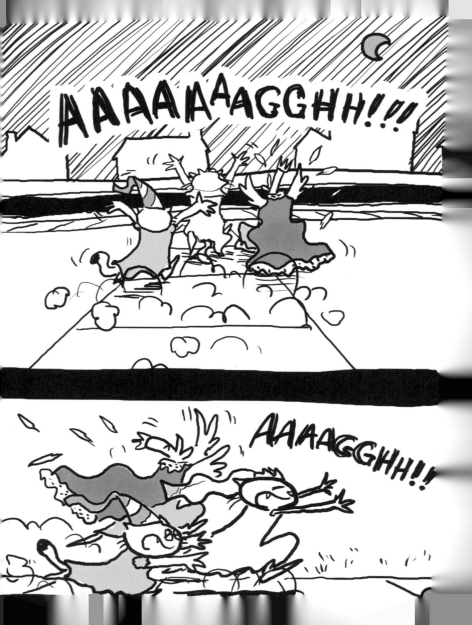

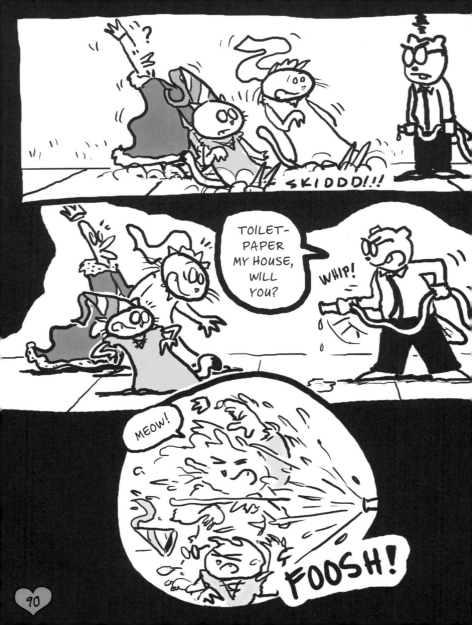

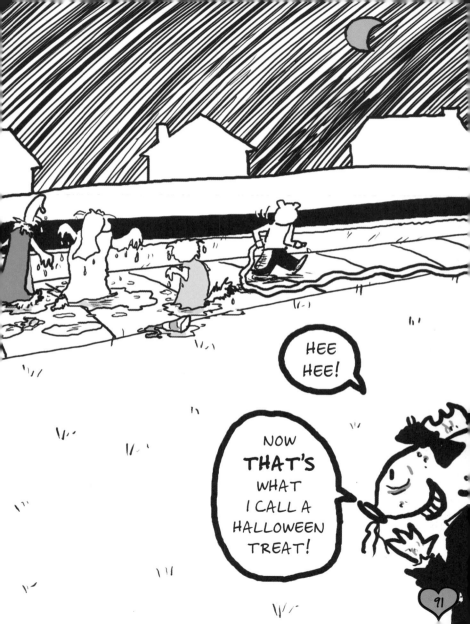

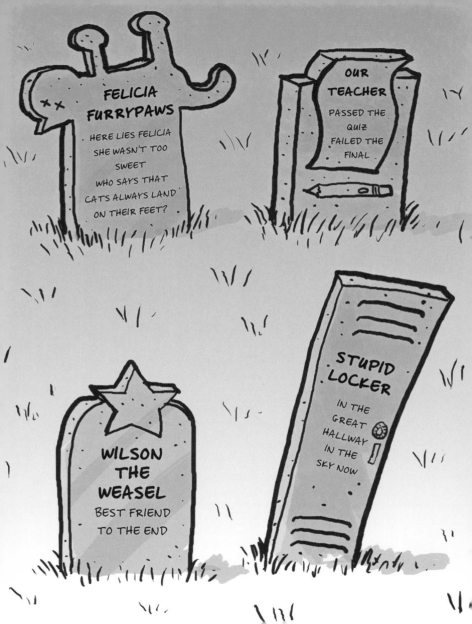

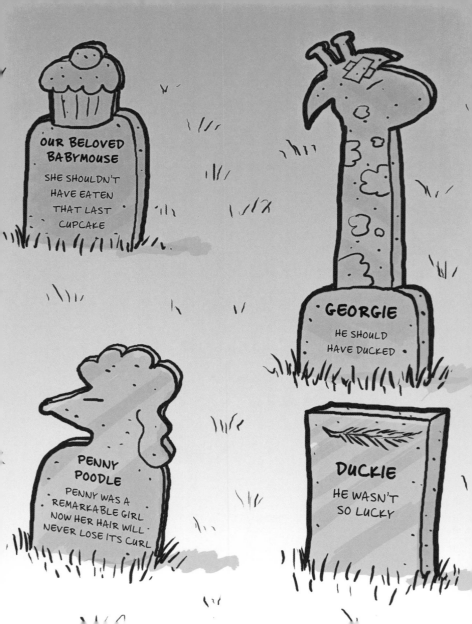

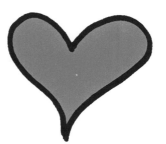

BABYMOUSE | IS HEADED TO | BROADWAY!

SNAP!

BABYMOUSE
THE MUSICAL

IF I CAN MAKE IT HERE, I CAN MAKE IT ANYWHERE!

COMING SPRING 2009!

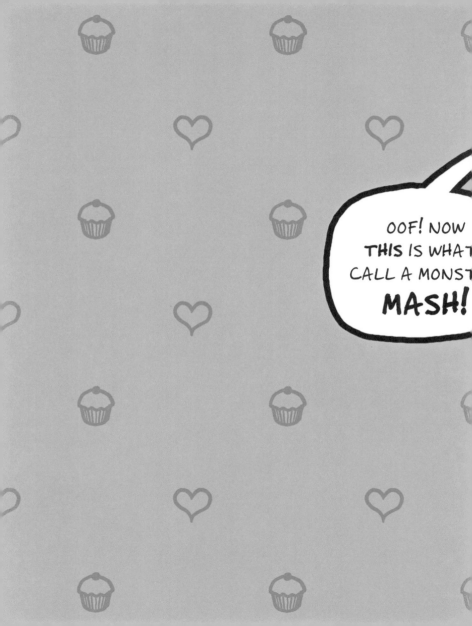

J-